Babies on the Go!

I raised two independent daughters with very different personalities. I am struck by the interesting journey they provided.

I bring this up because I was one of those children who loved to create clothing, accessories and imaginary lives for each one of my dolls. I assumed my daughters would follow suit. When my first daughter was old enough I created wonderful outfits, not only for her dolls, but for a few of her play ponies as well. Everything went as planned, and then my second daughter arrived.

She was encouraged by her older sister to participate, but somehow always managed to weave building bricks, animals and even fighting turtles into their imaginary stories. She had no desire to dress up anything, and that was OK. It is funny what our children teach us as we watch them grow.

Thank you girls for the journey, and please remember that if those fighting turtles ever need clothing for a special event, I might be persuaded to create the perfect outfit.

My hope is that you have as much fun creating clothes for your 10-inch doll as I did in selecting the fabrics for the designs in this book.

Sew far, sew good,

Lorine

Meet the Designer

Lorine Mason is an author, licensed artist, project designer and editor of the *Sewing Savvy* newsletter. Her work has been featured in print, on the Web and on television. She works with a variety of art mediums, combining them with her enthusiasm for all things fabric. She strives to create items others will be inspired to re-create, hopefully adding their own personal touches. Her creative career started in retail, weaving its way through management and education positions along the way. This experience, along with a goal to stay on top of trends in color and style, gives her current work the edge that manufacturers, publishers and editors have come to expect. She shares her life with her husband, Bill, and daughters, Jocelyn and Kimbrely in Virginia. ■

HOUSE of WHITE BIRCHES
PUBLISHERS SINCE 1947

Babies on the Go! is published by Annie's, 306 East Parr Road, Berne, IN 46711. Printed in USA. Copyright © 2012 Annie's. All rights reserved. This publication may not be reproduced in part or in whole without written permission from the publisher.

RETAIL STORES: If you would like to carry this pattern book or any other Annie's publications, visit AnniesWSL.com

Every effort has been made to ensure that the instructions in this pattern book are complete and accurate. We cannot, however, take responsibility for human error, typographical mistakes or variations in individual work. Please visit ClotildeCustomerCare.com to check for pattern updates.

ISBN: 978-1-59217-378-5
123456789

General Instructions

Fabric Selection

All of the outfits and accessories in this book were made using fat quarters. Available in colorful patterns and packaging, fat quarters are the "candy" in the fabric store and are a wonderful way to coordinate fabrics. Fat quarters are 18 x 22-inch cuts and are equivalent to standard 9 x 45-inch quarter yards. Any cotton fabric is suitable for these patterns.

Basic Sewing Supplies & Equipment

- Sewing machine and matching thread
- Scissors of various sizes, including pinking shears
- Rotary cutter(s), mats and straightedges
- Pattern-tracing paper or cloth
- Pressing tools such as sleeve rolls and June Tailor boards
- Pressing equipment, including ironing board and iron; press cloths
- Straight pins and pincushion
- Measuring tools
- Marking pens (either air- or water-soluble) or tailor's chalk
- Seam sealant
- Hand-sewing needles and thimble
- Point turners

Optional Supplies

- ¼-inch-wide double-sided basting tape
- Bias tape maker
- Tube-turning tool
- Mini-iron
- Serger

Construction & Application Techniques

Backstitching

Backstitch several stitches at the beginning and end of each seam to secure stitching. This ensures handling does not undo your seams.

Basting

Basting is a way to hold fabric pieces in place without using pins. It is especially useful in tight places or on small projects. Basting can be done by hand or machine using a longer-than-normal stitch length to sew where indicated. Remove basting stitches after garment is permanently sewn. Or, use a ¼-inch-wide basting tape.

Making Bias Tape

The following instructions are for making your own single-fold ¼-inch-wide bias tape if you do not wish to purchase it.

1. Fold fabric diagonally so crosswise grain straight edge is parallel to selvage or lengthwise grain. Cut fabric along this fold line to mark the true bias (Figure 1).

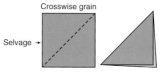

Figure 1

2. Using a clear ruler, mark successive bias lines 1 inch wide. Carefully cut along lines. Handle edges carefully to avoid stretching (Figure 2).

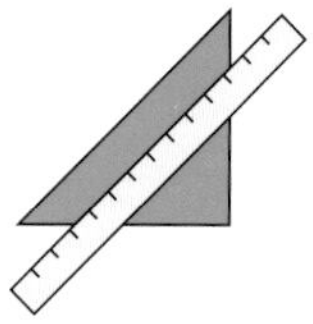

Figure 2

3. Sew short ends of strips together diagonally.

4. Fold strip in half lengthwise, wrong sides together and press.

5. Open flat with wrong side up. Fold each edge to center fold and press. Fold in half again and press (Figure 3).

Figure 3

Bias-Tape Bound Edges

1. Leaving bias tape folded, sandwich raw edges of garment between bias tape so the fabric raw edge meets the center fold of the bias tape (Figure 4).

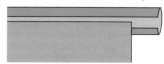

Figure 4

2. Edgestitch bias tape to secure (Figure 5). ***Note:*** *Purchased bias tape has one side wider than the other. Be sure to edgestitch with shorter side up when using purchased bias tape.*

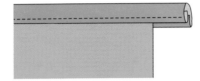

Figure 5

Bias-Tape Hem

1. Press center fold of bias tape flat, leaving edges folded (Figure 6).

Figure 6

2. Pin raw edge of bias tape along fabric raw edge and stitch in edge fold (Figure 7).

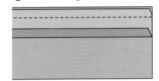

Figure 7

3. Press bias tape to wrong side and stitch along edge fold (Figure 8).

Figure 8

Bobbins

Fill multiple bobbins ahead of time with neutral colors of thread. Change only the top color of thread to either match or contrast with garment colors.

Double-Turned ¼-Inch Hem

1. Press ¼ inch to wrong side of section (Figure 9).

Figure 9

2. Turn and press again ¼ inch to wrong side. Edgestitch close to second fold (Figure 10).

Figure 10

Elastic Application

1. Cut elastic to specified length.

2. Position piece of elastic on the elastic placement line indicated on the pattern and pin at the side seam edges and at the middle. (Figure 11).

Figure 11

3. Position under machine needle and take a few stitches; backstitch to anchor elastic.

4. Gently stretch elastic between pins to same length as fabric, keeping elastic over placement line while stitching in place with a straight or zigzag stitch.

Elastic Waistline Casing

1. Create a waistline elastic casing by pressing fabric to the wrong side on the first fold line marked on the pattern.

2. Press fabric to the wrong side again on the marked casing fold line. Stitch close to the first fold line (Figure 12).

Figure 12

3. Thread elastic through the casing using a safety pin or bodkin attached to one end of the elastic.

4. Pin ends of elastic even with back seam. Stitch to secure (Figure 13).

Figure 13

5. Catch elastic ends in seam when completing the back seam.

Fastener Application

1. Try finished garment on doll to determine where fasteners should be positioned to fit doll's girth.

2. Mark position with pin, lapping one garment side over another (Figure 14).

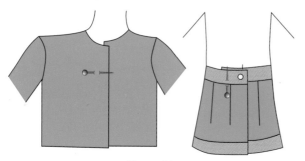

Figure 14

3. Apply fusible hook-and-loop tape to right and left sides of garment where marked using sizes indicated (Figure 15). Add decorative closures to right side of garment over hook-and-loop tape if desired.

Figure 15

Finishing Raw Edges

Every exposed seam should be finished for longer wear and cleaner construction. Finish raw edges with narrow zigzag or overcast stitches or by using a serger. Because of the garment sizes in this book, it is easier to finish raw edges prior to sewing the garment.

Gathering

1. Make two rows of longer-than-normal stitches on either side of the seam line, leaving long thread tails at either end (Figure 16).

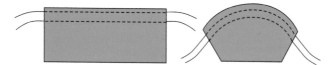

Figure 16

2. With right sides together, pin section to be gathered to appropriate garment section at each end and at the center (Figure 17).

Figure 17

3. Pull bobbin threads at one end to gather. When half of gathered section fits straight-edge length, secure bobbin threads by twisting around pin (Figure 18). Repeat for second half of section. Pin securely along seam line, adjusting gathers evenly.

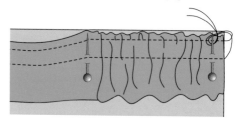

Figure 18

4. Stitch at seam line with gathered section on top (Figure 19). Keep gathers even so folds of fabric do not form while stitching.

Figure 19

5. Remove gathering stitches after sewing seam.

Single Hem

1. Press at least ¼ inch to wrong side of garment (Figure 20).

Figure 20

2. Measuring from the folded edge just made, press the hem width indicated in individual instructions to garment wrong side. (Figure 21).

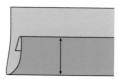

Figure 21

3. Edgestitch close to first fold (Figure 22).

Figure 22

4. If desired, use a contrasting thread to add a simple decorative finish to hems.

Sleeves

1. With right sides together, pin sleeve cap center to garment shoulder seam and edges of sleeve to garment sides (Figure 23). *Note: Placing the sleeve next to the sewing machine feed dogs will help ease any fullness into the seam.*

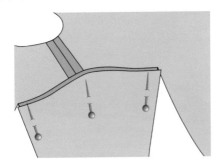

Figure 23

2. Stitch using a ¼-inch seam allowance. Press seam allowance toward sleeve (Figure 24).

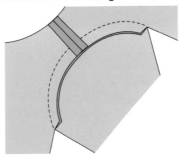

Figure 24

3. With right sides together, match armhole seams and pin underarm seam. Stitch using a ¼-inch seam allowance (Figure 25).

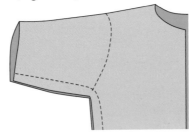

Figure 25

Topstitching

Topstitching provides a decorative touch while strengthening seams and edges. Because of the ¼-inch seams used in these projects, we suggest topstitching open seams from the wrong side. Stitch approximately ⅛ inch from the seam line or from the finished edge. ■

Sources

Page 6: Holiday Dress Up (Holiday Jumper and Blouse, All Decked Out, Christmas Romper)—Flurry collection by Kate Spain for Moda© www.unitednotions.com

Page 13: Play Date (Pool Side Suit, Cute Capri Set, Splash Pool Trunks)—Baby Geniuses Speak Up collection by Linda Carlson and Diana Henage for Benartex© www.benartex.com

Page 20: Sunday Dinner With Grandma (Ribbon & Roses Dress, Sassy Sundress, Little Man)—Floral Fancies collection by Beverly Maxvill for Benartex© www.bernartex.com

Page 28: Sleep Tight Little One (Snug as a Bug, Pretty in Pink, Cozy Pajamas)—Kashmir IV collection by Sentimental Studios for Moda© www.unitednotions.com

Fabric Fusion™ by Velcro© www.velcro.com

Berenguer© Lots to Love 10" dolls Clotilde.com

House of White Birches, Berne, Indiana 46711   Clotilde.com

Holiday Dress Up

Your dolls will be all decked out in these cute holiday outfits.

Holiday Jumper & Blouse

Materials

- 3 coordinating fat quarters (A, B, C)
- 8 inches ¼-inch-wide elastic
- 3 (¼-inch) coordinating buttons
- 1 package coordinating ¼-inch-wide single-fold bias tape
- 1¾ inches ¾-inch-wide fusible hook-and-loop tape
- Coordinating all-purpose thread
- Basic sewing supplies and equipment

Cutting

- Use pattern templates J1 and J2 and B1–B3 (pages 34 and 35). Transfer all pattern markings to fabric.

From fabric A:

- Fold fat quarter in half, right sides together.
- Cut one Jumper Front (J1) on the fold.
- Cut two Jumper Backs (J2).

From fabric B:

- Cut one 5 x 22-inch rectangle for skirt.

From fabric C:

- Fold fat quarter in half, right sides together.
- Cut one Blouse Front (B1) on fold.
- Cut two Blouse Backs (B2).
- Cut two Sleeves (B3) using long sleeve cutting line.

From fusible hook-and-loop tape:

- Cut three ¼ x 1¾-inch fasteners.

From elastic:

- Cut two 4-inch pieces for sleeves.

Assembly

Stitch right sides together using a ¼-inch seam allowance unless otherwise specified. Refer to General Instructions (page 2) for finishing all raw edges and for the following construction techniques: Bias-Tape Bound Edges, Gathering, Sleeves, Single Hem, Double-Turned ¼-Inch Hem, Elastic Application, Topstitching and Fastener Application.

Holiday Jumper

1. Fold Jumper Front (J1) wrong sides together at center fold. Stitch along placket seam line, ¼ inch from fold (Figure 1).

Figure 1

2. Open seam allowance and press flat to form a placket as shown in Figure 2.

Figure 2

3. Stitch front (J1) and back (J2) jumper pieces together at shoulder seams. Press seams toward back.

4. Bind neckline and armhole edges of jumper bodice using bias tape.

5. Stitch bodice side seams.

6. Stitch a ¾-inch Single Hem into one long edge of the 5 x 22-inch skirt rectangle.

7. Gather and stitch skirt to jumper bodice (Figure 3).

Figure 3

8. Stitch a Double-Turned ¼-Inch Hem along the back opening edges of the jumper.

9. Apply one fusible hook-and-loop tape fastener to the bodice back.

10. Position and stitch buttons evenly, centered on front placket (Figure 4).

Figure 4

Long-Sleeved Blouse

1. Stitch Blouse Front (B1) and Blouse Back (B2) together at shoulder seams; press seams toward back.

2. Bind neckline edge and Blouse Sleeve (B3) hemlines using bias tape.

3. Stitch a 4-inch piece of elastic on the elastic placement line of a sleeve. Repeat for second sleeve.

4. Stitch sleeves to blouse bodice matching shoulder seams to circle on sleeve cap.

5. Stitch underarm seam matching sleeve seams and notches and stopping stitching at circle.

6. Press ⅛ inch to wrong side along hemline and Topstitch.

7. Stitch Double-Turned ¼-Inch Hem along edges of Blouse Back.

8. Apply two fusible hook-and-loop tape fasteners to Blouse Back opening.

All Decked Out

Materials
- 3 coordinating fat quarters (A, B, C)
- 9 inches ¼-inch-wide elastic
- 1 package each ¼-inch-wide single-fold bias tape, coordinating with fabrics A and B
- 3 (¼-inch) coordinating buttons
- 1½ inches ¾-inch-wide fusible hook-and-loop tape
- Scrap fusible interfacing
- Coordinating all-purpose thread
- Basic sewing supplies and equipment

Cutting
- Use pattern templates S1–S4, B3, SV1, SV2 and CP1 (pages 35–38). Fold all fat quarters in half, right sides together. Transfer all pattern markings to fabric.

From fabric A:
- Use long sleeve cutting lines for all shirt and sleeve pieces.
- Cut one Shirt Back (S2) and one notched Shirt Collar (S3) on fold.
- Cut two Shirt Fronts (S1), two Facings (S4) and two Sleeves (B3).

From fabric B:
- Cut one Sweater Vest Back (SV2) on fold.
- Cut two Sweater Vest Fronts (SV1).

From fabric C:
- Cut two Capris/Pants (CP1), using pants cutting line and pattern markings.

From fusible hook-and-loop tape:
- Cut two ⅜ x 1½-inch fasteners.

From fusible interfacing:
- Cut two Facings (S4).

Assembly
Stitch right sides together using a ¼-inch seam allowance unless otherwise specified. Refer to General Instructions (page 2) for finishing all raw edges and for the following construction techniques: Bias-Tape Bound Edges, Sleeves, Double-Turned ¼-Inch Hem, Elastic Waistline Casing, Topstitching and Fastener Application.

Notched-Collar Shirt
1. Follow manufacturer's instructions and apply fusible interfacing to wrong side of Facings and finish curved and shoulder edges.

2. Stitch Facings to Shirt Fronts (Figure 1). Press seam toward Facings.

Figure 1

3. Stitch front and back shirt sections together at shoulder seams. Press seams open.

4. Fold notched collar in half lengthwise with right sides together and stitch short edges (Figure 2). Turn right side out, gently pushing collar tips out, and press. Topstitch around short ends and folded edge of collar.

Figure 2

5. Pin and baste notched collar to the neckline edge, matching collar ends to squares and center back notches referring to Figure 3.

Figure 3

6. Fold front facings back along seam over the collar ends matching shoulder seams.

7. Lightly press open 5 inches of bias tape, leaving one edge folded. Center and pin right side of unfolded bias edge to Shirt Back neckline, over Shirt Collar and Facing referring to Figure 4.

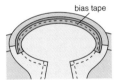

bias tape

Figure 4

8. Stitch through all layers. Remove collar basting. Clip curves, turn right side out and press.

9. Bind the hem edges of sleeves and Shirt Fronts and Back using bias tape. Begin binding at circles on side seams for Shirt Fronts and Back referring to Figure 5.

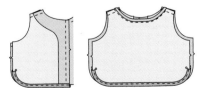

Figure 5

10. Topstitch along center front and neckline edges of shirt, close to edges and ³⁄₈ inch from edge as shown in Figure 6.

Figure 6

11. Stitch sleeves to shirt.

12. Beginning at circle, sew side seams of shirt matching underarm seams and notches.

13. Apply fusible hook-and-loop tape fastener to the shirt opening.

Pants

1. Fold and press along pants front fold line. Stitch ⅛ inch from fold to make center front tuck (Figure 7).

Figure 7

2. Stitch center front pants seam, referring to Figure 8. Press seam to one side and Topstitch in place.

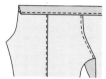

Figure 8

3. Stitch a Double-Turned ¼-Inch Hem along bottom edge of each of the pant legs.

4. Create an Elastic Waistline Casing as shown in Figure 8. Thread elastic through the casing, pinning ends of elastic even with the fabric edges.

5. Stitch pant center back seam. Press to one side and Topstitch in place.

6. Sew inner leg seams to complete pants.

Sweater Vest

1. Stitch shoulder seams of vest and press seams open.

2. Bind armhole edges using bias tape.

3. Stitch vest side seams and press open.

4. Bind all remaining edges of vest using bias tape, beginning and ending along the center back.

5. Apply fusible hook-and-loop tape fastener to Vest Fronts.

6. Sew three buttons to vest left front referring to pattern markings.

Christmas Romper

Materials

- 3 coordinating fat quarters (A, B, C)
- 20 inches ¼-inch-wide elastic
- 2 (¼-inch) coordinating buttons
- 1 package coordinating ¼-inch-wide single-fold bias tape
- 1½ inches ¾-inch-wide fusible hook-and-loop tape
- Coordinating all-purpose thread
- Basic sewing supplies and equipment

Cutting

- Use pattern templates R1, R2 and B1—B3 (pages 34, 35 and 39). Fold fat quarters in half, right sides together. Transfer all pattern markings to fabric.

From fabric A:

- Cut one Romper Yoke (R1) on fold.
- Cut two Romper Pants (R2).
- Cut one 1 x 10-inch strip for shoulder straps.

From fabric B:

- Cut one Romper Yoke (R1) for lining on fold.
- Cut two 2½ x 18-inch strips for ruffle.

From fabric C:

- Cut one Blouse Front (B1) on fold.
- Cut two Blouse Backs (B2).
- Cut two Sleeves (B3) using long sleeve cutting line.

From fusible hook-and-loop tape:

- Cut one ¼ x 1-inch fastener.
- Cut one ¼ x 1¾-inch fastener.
- Cut two ¼-inch squares from remainder.

From elastic:

- Cut two ¼ x 4-inch pieces for sleeves.
- Cut two ¼ x 6-inch pieces for pants legs.

Assembly

Stitch right sides together using a ¼-inch seam allowance unless otherwise specified. Refer to General Instructions (page 2) for finishing all seams and for the following construction techniques: Bias-Tape Bound Edges, Gathering, Sleeves, Double-Turned ¼-Inch Hem, Elastic Application, Topstitching and Fastener Application.

Christmas Romper

1. Fold both short ends of shoulder strap strip to wrong side ¼ inch and press.

2. Fold shoulder strap in half lengthwise, right sides together and stitch using ⅛-inch seam. Turn right side out, cut strip in half to make two 5-inch-long shoulder straps. Press flat with seam centered on wrong side. Edgestitch all sides of the shoulder straps.

3. Position and pin raw edge of shoulder straps on squares on Romper Yoke (R1) back matching raw edges right sides together (Figure 1).

Figure 1

4. Stitch fabric A and B Romper Yokes (R1) top edges, armholes and back seams right sides together, catching shoulder straps in the seam.

5. Clip curves and trim corners as shown in Figure 2. Turn right side out, pulling shoulder straps away from yoke and press.

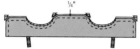

Figure 2

6. Cut one 2½ x 18-inch ruffle in half to make two 9-inch lengths. Stitch 9-inch pieces to short ends of second ruffle. Press seams open.

7. Fold ruffle in half lengthwise, right sides together. Stitch short ends together. Trim corners, turn right side out and press flat.

8. Gather and stitch ruffle to Romper Yoke bottom edge.

9. Stitch center back seam of Romper Pants, stopping stitching at circle (Figure 3).

Figure 3

10. Stitch a Double-Turned ¼-Inch Hem along center back edges of Romper Pants from circle to top edge (Figure 4).

Figure 4

11. Stitch center front seam of Romper Pants.

12. Bias-bind bottom edge of pants legs.

13. Stitch a 6-inch piece of elastic to pants along elastic placement line.

14. Stitch the romper pants to ruffled yoke edge.

15. Stitch inner pants leg seam matching center front and back seams and bound hem edges.

16. Apply ¼ x 1-inch fusible hook-and-loop tape fastener to center back opening. Apply ¼-inch hook-and-loop tape squares to wrong side of shoulder strap ends and front of yoke.

17. Sew a button to right side of the end of each shoulder strap.

Long-Sleeved Blouse

1. Stitch Blouse Front (B1) and Blouse Back (B2) together at shoulder seams; press seams toward back.

2. Bind neckline edge and Blouse Sleeve (B3) hemlines using bias tape.

3. Stitch a 4-inch piece of elastic on the elastic placement line of a sleeve. Repeat for second sleeve.

4. Stitch sleeves to blouse bodice matching shoulder seams to circle on sleeve cap.

5. Stitch underarm seam, matching sleeve seams and notches and stopping stitching at circle.

6. Press ⅛ inch to wrong side along hemline and Topstitch.

7. Stitch Double-Turned ¼-Inch Hem along edges of Blouse Back.

8. Apply ¼ x 1¾-inch piece fusible hook-and-loop tape fastener to Blouse Back opening. ■

Play Date

Dress your dolls for a fun play date in these poolside fashions or a cute Capri set.

Poolside Suit

Materials
- 2 coordinating fat quarters (A, B)
- 1 package coordinating ¼-inch-wide single-fold bias tape
- 12 inches ¼-inch-wide elastic
- 1 (¾-inch) fish character button
- ½ x ¾-inch fusible hook-and-loop tape
- Coordinating all-purpose thread
- Basic sewing supplies and equipment

Cutting
- Use pattern templates BS1, BS2 and C3–C5 (pages 40 and 41). Fold all fat quarters in half, right sides together. Transfer all pattern markings to fabric.

From fabric A:
- Cut one Bathing Suit Top (BS1) on fold.
- Cut four Bathing Suit Bottoms (BS2).

From fabric B:
- Cut one Cover-Up Back (C4) on fold.
- Cut two Cover-Up Fronts (C3).
- Cut two Cover-Up Pockets (C5).

From elastic:
- Cut one each 8-inch and 4-inch piece.

Assembly
Stitch right sides together using a ¼-inch seam allowance unless otherwise specified. Refer to General Instructions (page 2) for finishing all raw edges and for the following construction techniques: Bias-Tape Bound Edges, Double-Turned ¼-Inch Hem, Elastic Waistline Casing, Elastic Application, Topstitching and Fastener Application.

Bathing Suit
1. Bind the top and bottom edges of the Bathing Suit Top using bias tape.

2. Stitch Double-Turned ¼-Inch Hem on Bathing Suit Top ends.

3. Apply fusible hook-and-loop tape fastener to the Bathing Suit Top ends to complete.

4. Stitch side seams of Bathing Suit Bottom. Press seams open.

5. Bind the leg hems of Bathing Suit Bottom using bias tape.

6. Stitch center front seam of Bathing Suit Bottom (Figure 1). Press seam to one side.

Figure 1

7. Make an Elastic Waistline Casing and thread an 8-inch piece of elastic through the casing, pinning ends of elastic even with the fabric edges.

8. Stitch center back seam.

9. Stitch inner leg seam to complete Bathing Suit Bottom.

Sleeveless Cover-Up

1. Fold cover-up back, right sides together at center back, and stitch on marked tuck stitching line.

2. Press tuck to left side and Topstitch down 1½ inches; pivot and stitch to end of tuck stitching line at an angle as shown in Figure 2.

Figure 2

3. Stitch shoulder seams together and press open.

4. Bind armholes, back hemline between small squares, and around all front edges between small squares using bias tape (Figure 3).

Figure 3

5. Apply a 4-inch piece of elastic along elastic placement line on cover-up back.

6. Cut two 8-inch pieces of bias tape and edgestitch the folded edges together to make cover-up ties.

7. Position and pin a tie end to each side seam, just above the elastic on the right side (Figure 4).

Figure 4

8. Stitch side seams of the cover-up catching ends of ties in seam, ending at large square. Press open.

9. Stitch pocket pieces right sides together, leaving a 1-inch opening for turning.

10. Turn right side out, turning opening seam allowances inside and press.

11. Position pocket on right front side, matching small and large dots.

12. Topstitch pocket to the cover-up (Figure 5).

Figure 5

13. Attach fish character button to the right front side above pocket.

Cute Capri Set

Materials

- 2 coordinating fat quarters (A, B)
- 1 package coordinating ¼-inch-wide single-fold bias tape
- 8 inches ¼-inch-wide elastic
- 4 (¼-inch) coordinating plastic buttons
- ⅜ x 1½-inch-wide fusible hook-and-loop tape
- Coordinating all-purpose thread
- Basic sewing supplies and equipment

Cutting

- Use pattern templates J1, J2 and CP1 (pages 35 and 38). Fold fat quarter in half, right sides together. Transfer all pattern markings to fabric.

From fabric A:
- Cut one Jumper Front (J1) on fold.
- Cut two Jumper Backs (J2).
- Cut two 1 x 7-inch strips for Capri cuffs.

From fabric B:
- Cut two Capri/Pants (CP1), using Capri cutting line.
- Cut one 2½ x 18-inch strip for Ruffled Top ruffle.

Assembly

Stitch right sides together using a ¼-inch seam allowance unless otherwise specified. Refer to General Instructions (page 2) for finishing all raw edges and for the following construction techniques: Bias-Tape Bound Edges, Gathering, Double-Turned ¼-Inch Hem, Elastic Waistline Casing, Topstitching and Fastener Application.

Ruffled Top

1. Stitch Jumper Front (J1) and Jumper Back (J2) pieces together at shoulder seams. Press seams open.

2. Bind neckline, armhole edges and one long edge of ruffle using bias tape.

3. Stitch jumper side seams together. Press seams open.

4. Gather ruffle and stitch to the bottom edge of jumper. Press seam toward jumper. Topstitch through all layers.

5. Stitch a Double-Turned ¼-Inch Hem along both sides of top back opening.

6. Use a double-threaded needle to gather both shoulder seams (Figure 1).

Figure 1

7. Sew one ¼-inch button on each shoulder over gathering, again referring to Figure 1.

8. Apply fusible hook-and-loop tape fastener to top back opening.

Capris

1. Press ¼ inch to wrong side of one long edge of a Capri cuff. Repeat on second cuff.

2. Stitch right side of a Capri cuff to wrong side of a Capri pant leg, matching raw edge of cuff to Capri hem edge (Figure 2).

Figure 2

3. Press and pin cuff to right side encasing the seam. Topstitch along cuff fold as shown in Figure 2.

4. Stitch center front seam. Press seam to one side and Topstitch.

5. Make an Elastic Waistline Casing and thread elastic through the casing, pinning ends of elastic even with the fabric edges.

6. Stitch center back seam. Press seam to one side and Topstitch.

7. Stitch inner leg seam.

8. Use a double-threaded needle to gather pant leg cuffs at sides referring to step 6 of Ruffled Top and Figure 3.

Figure 3

9. Sew a button over gathers on each leg.

House of White Birches, Berne, Indiana 46711   Clotilde.com

Splash Pool Trunks

Materials
- 3 coordinating fat quarters (A, B, C)
- 1 package coordinating ¼-inch-wide single-fold bias tape
- 9 inches ¼-inch-wide elastic
- 3 (¼-inch) coordinating buttons
- ⅜ x 1½-inch piece fusible hook-and-loop tape
- Coordinating all-purpose thread
- Basic sewing supplies and equipment

Cutting
- Use pattern templates SP1–SP3, S1–S3 and B3 (pages 35, 36 and 42). Fold fat quarter in half, right sides together. Transfer all pattern markings to fabric.

From fabric A:
- Use short sleeve cutting lines for all shirt and sleeve pieces.
- Cut one Shirt Back (S2) and one Regular Collar (S3) on fold.
- Cut two each Shirt Fronts (S1) and Sleeves (B3).

From fabric B:
- Cut two Swim Trunks (SP1) on fold.

From fabric C:
- Cut two each Swim Trunks Pocket (SP2) and Swim Trunks Pocket Flap (SP3).

Assembly
Stitch right sides together using a ¼-inch seam allowance unless otherwise specified. Refer to General Instructions (page 2) for finishing all raw edges and for the following construction techniques: Double-Turned ¼-Inch Hem, Elastic Waistline Casing, Bias-Tape Hem, Topstitching and Fastener Application.

Bathing Trunks
1. Stitch a Bias Tape Hem in Swim Trunks legs.

2. Make a Double-Turned ¼-Inch Hem on top of Pockets. Press sides and bottoms ¼ inch to wrong side.

3. Position Pockets on Swim Trunks sides matching large and small circles. Topstitch sides and bottoms (Figure 1).

4. Fold Pocket Flaps in half right sides together and stitch short sides.

5. Turn right side out; press. Topstitch short sides and folded edges.

6. Position and pin Pocket Flaps above Pockets, matching small squares as shown in Figure 2. Stitch ¼ inch from raw edge.

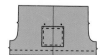

Figure 1

Figure 2

7. Press flap toward Pocket and Topstitch across the top edge of the Pocket Flap, again referring to Figure 2.

8. Stitch center front seam; press seam to one side.

9. Make an Elastic Waistline Casing and thread elastic through the casing, pinning ends of elastic even with the fabric edges.

10. Stitch center back seam catching elastic in seam; press seam to one side.

11. Stitch inner leg seam.

Short-Sleeved Shirt

1. Stitch front (S1) and back (S2) sections together at shoulder seams; press seams open.

2. Cut two 3-inch pieces of bias tape. Press center fold of bias tape flat, leaving edges folded. Pin raw edge of bias tape along shirt front raw edges and stitch in edge fold. Refer to steps 1 and 2 of Bias-Tape Hems in General Instructions on page 3.

3. Fold regular collar in half lengthwise with right sides together and stitch short edges (Figure 3). Turn right side out, gently pushing collar tips out, and press.

Figure 3

4. Pin and baste regular collar to the neckline edge, matching center back notches and collar ends to center fronts referring to Figure 4.

Figure 4

5. Fold front bias tape back along seam over the collar ends.

6. Cut an 8-inch piece of bias tape. Press center fold of bias tape flat, leaving edges folded. Pin raw edge of bias tape along neckline edge over collar and extending past front bias tape (Figure 5). Stitch in edge fold.

Figure 5

7. Clip curves, turn right side out and press.

8. Edgestitch on wrong side of shirt along both sides of binding, around the neckline and down the shirt fronts as shown in Figure 6.

Figure 6

9. Stitch a Double-Turned ¼-Inch Hem on short-sleeve hem edges.

10. Stitch sleeves to the shirt. Press armhole seam toward sleeve and Topstitch close to the seam (Figure 7).

Figure 7

11. Stitch side seams.

12. Stitch a Bias-Tape Hem at shirt hemline. Topstitch along hemline.

13. Apply fusible hook-and-loop tape fastener to shirt fronts.

14. Sew buttons spaced evenly to left front opening. ■

Sunday Dinner With Grandma

These three "dressy" outfits are adorable from top to bottom.
They are perfect for Sunday dinner with Grandma.

Sassy Sundress

Materials
- 3 coordinating fat quarters (A, B, C)
- 9 inches ¼-inch-wide elastic
- 8 inches ⅛-inch-wide elastic
- ½ x 1¼-inch fusible hook-and-loop tape
- Coordinating all-purpose thread
- Basic sewing supplies and equipment

Cutting
- Use pattern templates P1 and SD1 (page 43). Transfer all pattern markings to fabric.

From fabric A:
- Cut two Sundress Bodices (SD1).
- Cut two 1½ x 4-inch strips for shoulder straps.
- Cut two Pantaloons (P1).

From fabric B:
- Cut two 8 x 18-inch strips for skirt.

From fabric C:
- Cut two 1¼ x 12½-inch strips for waistband.
- Cut one 1 x 16-inch strip for binding.

Assembly

Stitch right sides together using a ¼-inch seam allowance unless otherwise specified. Refer to General Instructions (page 2) for finishing all raw edges and for the following construction techniques: Elastic Waistline Casing, Bias-Tape Bound Edges, Topstitching, Gathering, Elastic Application and Fastener Application.

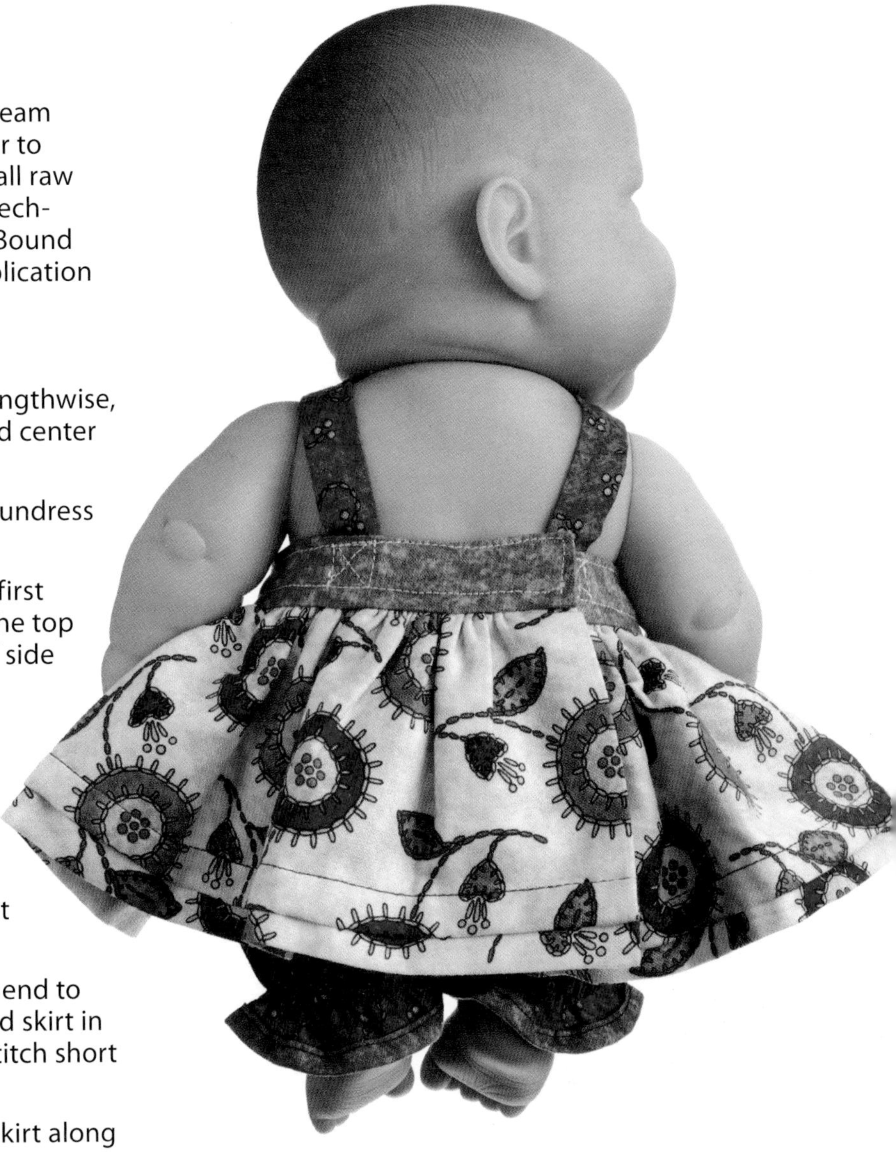

Sundress

1. Fold and stitch shoulder straps in half lengthwise, right sides together. Turn right side out and center seam on back. Press flat and finish ends.

2. Position and pin straps to right side of Sundress Bodice (SD1) at squares.

3. Position second bodice piece on top of first bodice, right sides together. Stitch along the top and sides of bodice, keeping straps free of side seams (Figure 1).

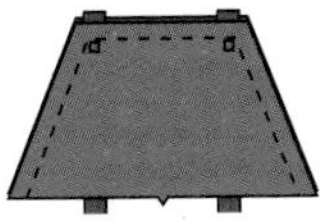

Figure 1

4. Carefully clip corners. Turn right side out and press.

5. Stitch skirt strips together on one short end to make one long strip; press seam open. Fold skirt in half lengthwise right sides together and stitch short ends. Turn right side out and press.

6. Fold and press 1 inch to wrong side of skirt along pressed long edge. Stitch ¼ inch from fold line and press fold toward bottom edge of skirt as seen in Figure 2.

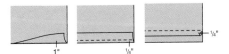

Figure 2

7. Mark lengthwise center of both waistband strips. Finish one long edge of one waistband strip.

8. Position and pin bodice notched edge between waistband strips, right sides together, matching raw edges and waistband center to notch (Figure 3). Stitch waistband together at short ends and along pinned edge catching bodice in seam.

Figure 3

9. Gather raw edges of skirt and stitch right sides together to unfinished waistband edge, matching skirt center seam to waistband center.

10. Press waistband away from skirt. Pull finished edge of waistband over seam allowances, enclosing seam in waistband, and pin on right side (Figure 4).

Figure 4

11. Topstitch ⅛ inch from all edges of waistband as shown in Figure 5.

Figure 5

12. Topstitch straps 1¼ inches from either waistband end, stitching a square with an X inside as shown in Figure 6.

Figure 6

13. Apply fusible hook-and-loop tape fastener to the waistband of the sundress.

Pantaloons

1. Bind pantaloon leg hem edges using binding strip from fabric C.

2. Apply 4-inch strips of ⅛-inch elastic to each pantaloon leg on marked placement line.

3. Stitch center front seam of pantaloons.

4. Make an Elastic Waistline Casing and thread 9-inch length of ¼-inch-wide elastic through the casing, pinning ends of elastic even with the fabric edges.

5. Stitch pantaloon center back seam.

6. Stitch inner leg seam.

Ribbon & Roses Dress

Materials
- 3 coordinating fat quarters (A, B, C)
- 19 inches ¼-inch-wide elastic
- 8 inches ⅛-inch-wide elastic
- 6 miniature fabric roses
- ⅜ x 1¾-inch piece fusible hook-and-loop tape
- Coordinating all-purpose thread
- Basic sewing supplies and equipment

Cutting
- Use pattern templates D1–D3 and P1 (pages 43 and 44). Transfer all pattern markings to fabric.

From fabric A:
- Fold fat quarter in half right sides together.
- Cut one Dress Bodice Front (D1) on fold.
- Cut two each Dress Bodice Back (D2) and Dress Sleeve (D3).
- Cut two 4 x 18-inch strips for skirt.

From fabric B:
- Cut one 1½ x 22-inch strip for belt.
- Refer to Making Bias Tape in General Instructions on page 2, cut 1-inch-wide bias strips to total at least 32 inches.

From fabric C:
- Cut two Pantaloons (P1).
- Cut one 1¼ x 22-inch strip for Headband.

From elastic:
- Cut one 9-inch and one 10-inch length piece from ¼-inch-wide elastic.
- Cut two 4-inch length pieces from ⅛-inch-wide elastic.

Assembly
Stitch right sides together using a ¼-inch seam allowance unless otherwise specified. Refer to General Instructions (page 2) for finishing all raw edges and for the following construction techniques: Bias-Tape Bound Edges, Sleeves, Gathering, Double-Turned ¼-Inch Hem, Elastic Waistline Casing, Elastic Application and Fastener Application.

Ribbon & Roses Dress
1. Stitch Dress Bodice Front (D1) and Backs (D2) together at shoulder seams; press seams open.

2. Bind neckline edge and sleeve hem edges using fabric B binding strip.

3. Stitch sleeves to bodice of dress.

4. Stitch underarm and side seams.

5. Stitch two skirt strips together along short ends; press seam to one side.

6. Press and stitch a Double-Turned ¼-Inch Hem along bottom edge of skirt.

7. Gather and stitch skirt to bodice matching center front notch to skirt seam.

8. Press and stitch a Double-Turned ¼-Inch Hem along back opening of dress.

9. Fold belt strip in half lengthwise right sides together and stitch. Turn right side out, center seam on back side and press (Figure 1).

Figure 1

10. Turn and press one raw edge of belt to wrong side. Center pressed edge of belt over waistline on wrong side of dress left side back opening; hand-stitch in place (Figure 2).

Figure 2

11. Hand-tack the belt at side seams centered on waistline seam.

12. Tie a bow even with right back opening edge. Trim belt length to approximately ½ inch past opening edge. Turn excess belt length ¼ inch to wrong side. Fold belt end to wrong side of dress and hand-stitch in place, centered over the waistline seam (Figure 3).

Figure 3

13. Stitch three mini roses to the belt at center front, sewing through all layers of fabric.

14. Apply fusible hook-and-loop tape fastener to the back bodice opening above the belt.

Pantaloons

1. Bind Pantaloon leg hem edges using fabric B binding strip.

2. Apply 4-inch strips of ⅛-inch-wide elastic to Pantaloon leg on marked placement line.

3. Stitch center front seam of Pantaloons.

4. Make an Elastic Waistline Casing and thread 9-inch length of ¼-inch-wide elastic through the casing, pinning ends of elastic even with the fabric edges.

5. Stitch Pantaloon center back seam catching elastic.

6. Stitch inner leg seam.

Headband

1. Fold and press one short end of the Headband strip to the wrong side ¼ inch and then in half lengthwise right sides together. Stitch along length, leaving ends open to make a tube.

2. Turn right side out and press. Insert a 10-inch length of elastic into the fabric tube. Overlap elastic ends and stitch to secure.

3. Insert raw end of tube into pressed end of tube and stitch to secure.

4. Trim around the edges of the bow using pinking shears and rounding both ends.

5. Wrap the fabric strip around the seam of the Headband and tie a knot to make a bow on the band.

Little Man

Materials
- 3 coordinating fat quarters (A, B, C)
- 1 package ¼-inch-wide single-fold bias binding
- 9-inch piece ¼-inch-wide elastic
- 4 (¼-inch) coordinating buttons
- 3 inches fusible hook-and-loop tape
- Basic sewing supplies and equipment

Cutting
- Use pattern templates S1–S3, S5, B3, CP1, V1 and V2 (pages 35, 36, 38 and 45). Fold all fat quarters in half lengthwise with right sides together. Transfer all pattern markings to fabric.

From fabric A:
- Use long sleeve cutting lines for all shirt and sleeve pieces.
- Cut one each Shirt Back (S2) and Regular Shirt Collar (S3) on fold.
- Cut two each Shirt Front (S1) and Blouse Sleeves (B3).
- Cut one Pocket (S5).

From fabric B:
- Cut one Vest Back (V1) on fold.
- Cut two Vest Fronts (V2).

From fabric C:
- Cut one Vest Back (V1) on fold for lining.
- Cut two Vest Fronts (V2) for lining.
- Cut two Capris/Pants (CP1) using Pants cutting line.

From fusible hook-and-loop tape:
- Cut two ⅜ x 1½-inch fasteners.

Assembly
Stitch right sides together using a ¼-inch seam allowance unless otherwise specified. Refer to General Instructions (page 2) for finishing all raw edges and for the following construction techniques: Sleeves, Double-Turned ¼-Inch Hem, Elastic Casing, Topstitching and Fastener Application.

Long-Sleeved Shirt
1. Stitch Shirt Front (S1) and Back (S2) sections together at shoulder seams; press seams open.

2. Cut two 4-inch pieces of bias tape. Press center fold of bias tape flat, leaving edges folded. Pin raw edge of bias tape along center front raw edges and stitch in edge fold. Refer to steps 1 and 2 of Bias-Tape Hems in General Instructions page 3.

3. Fold Regular Shirt Collar in half lengthwise with right sides together and stitch short edges (Figure 1). Turn right side out, gently pushing collar tips out, and press. Topstitch around ends and folded edge of collar.

Figure 1

4. Pin and baste regular collar to the neckline edge matching center back notches and collar ends to center fronts referring to Figure 2.

Figure 2

5. Fold front bias tape back along seam over the collar ends.

6. Cut an 8-inch piece of bias tape. Press center fold of bias tape flat, leaving edges folded. Pin raw edge of bias tape along neckline edge over collar and extending past front bias tape (Figure 3). Stitch in edge fold.

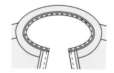

Figure 3

7. Clip curves, turn right side out and press.

8. Edgestitch on wrong side of shirt along both sides of bias tape, around the neckline and down the Shirt Fronts as shown in Figure 4.

Figure 4

9. Fold and press ¼ inch to wrong side on Pocket (S5) top straight edge and stitch along raw edge.

10. Fold and press ¼ inch to wrong side on remaining sides of pocket. Position and pin pocket to shirt left front at circles. Edgestitch around pocket sides and bottom.

11. Stitch a Double-Turned ¼-Inch Hem on short-sleeve hem edges.

12. Stitch sleeves to the shirt. Press armhole seam toward sleeve.

13. Beginning at circle, stitch side seams matching notches.

14. Fold and press shirt hem edge ⅛ inch to wrong side and Topstitch.

15. Apply fusible hook-and-loop tape fastener to Shirt Fronts.

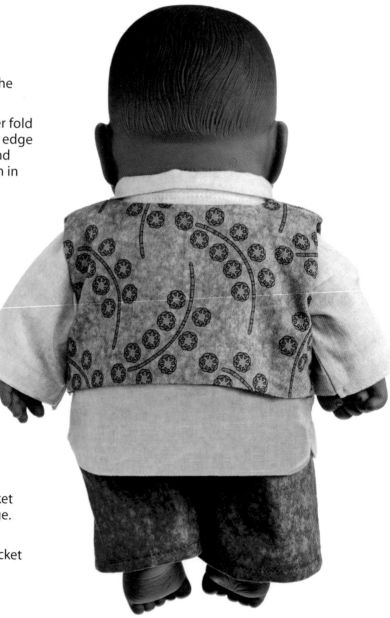

Pants

1. Stitch center front pants seam. Press seam to one side and Topstitch in place.

2. Stitch a Double-Turned ¼-Inch Hem along bottom edge of each of the pant legs.

3. Create an Elastic Waistline Casing and thread elastic through the casing, pinning ends of elastic even with the fabric edges.

4. Stitch pant center back seam; press to one side.

5. Sew inner leg seams to complete pants.

Vest

1. Stitch Vest Front (V2) and Back (V1) fabric pieces together at shoulder seams and Vest Front and Back lining pieces together at shoulder seams.

2. With right sides together, stitch vest and vest lining together at sleeve openings, around neckline and bottom edges (Figure 5). Leave underarm seams open.

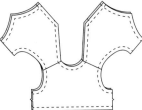

Figure 5

3. Clip curves, turn right side out and press.

4. Turn Vest Back side seam openings ¼ inch to inside. Insert the front side seams into back side seams and Topstitch the seams closed as shown in Figure 6.

Figure 6

5. Apply fusible hook-and-loop tape fastener to the front of the Vest.

6. Sew buttons centered evenly along center left front edge. ◼

Sleep Tight Little One

Use soft pastel print fabrics for this cute sleeping bag, nightgown and pajamas, and your doll will be ready for a good night's sleep.

Snug as a Bug

Materials

- 2 coordinating fat quarters (A, B)
- Coordinating fabric scrap
- ½ yard ¼-inch-wide elastic
- 1 package fusible batting
- Polyester stuffing scraps
- Coordinating all-purpose thread
- Basic sewing supplies and equipment

Cutting

- Use pattern templates SB1 and SB2 (pages 46 and 47). Fold fat quarters in half right sides together lengthwise. Transfer all pattern markings to fabric.

From fabric A:

- Cut one each Sleeping Bag Back (SB1) and Sleeping Bag Front (SB2) on fold.
- Cut two 2 x 18-inch strips for binding.
- Cut one 1½ x 5-inch rectangle for bow.

From fabric B:

- Cut one each Sleeping Bag Back (SB1) and Sleeping Bag Front (SB2) on fold.
- Cut one 2½ x 18-inch strip for ruffle.
- Cut one 2½ x 14-inch strip for Headband.

From coordinating fabric scrap:

- Cut one 2½ x 3½-inch rectangle for pillow.

From fusible batting:

- Cut one each Sleeping Bag Back (SB1) and Sleeping Bag Front (SB2) on fold.

From elastic:

- Cut one 7½-inch length for Sleeping Bag.
- Cut one 10-inch length for Headband.

Assembly

Stitch right sides together using a ¼-inch seam allowance unless otherwise specified. Refer to General Instructions (page 2) for finishing all raw edges and for the following construction techniques: Gathering and Topstitching.

Sleeping Bag

1. Layer fabric B Sleeping Bag Back right side down, batting and fabric A Sleeping Bag Back right side up. Pin-baste layers together (Figure 1).

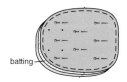

Figure 1

2. Beginning at center of Sleeping Bag Back, stitch lines 1 inch apart vertically to quilt back (Figure 2). Remove pins.

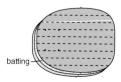

Figure 2

3. Fold and press the 2½ x 18-inch ruffle strip in half lengthwise, wrong sides together. Gather and stitch ruffle to top edge of fabric A Sleeping Bag Front top straight edge (Figure 3).

Figure 3

4. Layer batting, fabric A Sleeping Bag Front right side up and fabric B Sleeping Bag Front right side down. Pin and stitch ½ inch from top straight edge as shown in Figure 4.

Figure 4

5. Turn fabric B layer over to batting side, pulling ruffle up and away from seam; press.

6. Topstitch ⅜ inch from seam to form an elastic casing. Continue stitching horizontally to the casing seam, 1 inch apart, to quilt the Sleeping Bag Front (Figure 5).

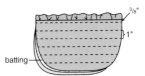

Figure 5

7. Thread 7½-inch length of elastic through the casing, stitching across ends to secure.

8. Gather and pin Sleeping Bag Front fabric B side to Sleeping Bag Back fabric A side, matching notches and adjusting gathers evenly. Stitch a ⅜-inch seam around outside edge.

9. Press all raw edges of pillow ¼ inch to wrong side.

10. Position pillow corners at dots on Sleeping Bag Back and Topstitch through all layers leaving a 2-inch opening along one edge.

11. Lightly stuff the pillow with polyester fiberfill, stuffing scraps through opening; stitch the opening closed.

12. Join binding strips on short ends with diagonal seams to make one long strip; trim seams to ¼ inch and press seams open.

13. Fold and press the binding strip in half with wrong sides together along length.

14. Sew binding to Sleeping Bag outer edges, matching raw edges and overlapping ends.

15. Fold binding to the back side and hand-stitch in place to finish.

Headband

1. Fold and press one short end of the Headband strip to the wrong side ¼ inch and then in half lengthwise right sides together. Stitch along length, leaving ends open to make a tube.

2. Turn right side out and press. Insert a 10-inch length of elastic into the fabric tube. Overlap elastic ends and stitch to secure (Figure 6).

Figure 6

3. Insert raw end of tube into pressed end of tube and stitch to secure (Figure 7).

Figure 7

4. Trim around the edges of the bow using pinking shears and rounding both ends.

5. Wrap the fabric strip around the seam of the Headband and tie a knot to make a bow on the band.

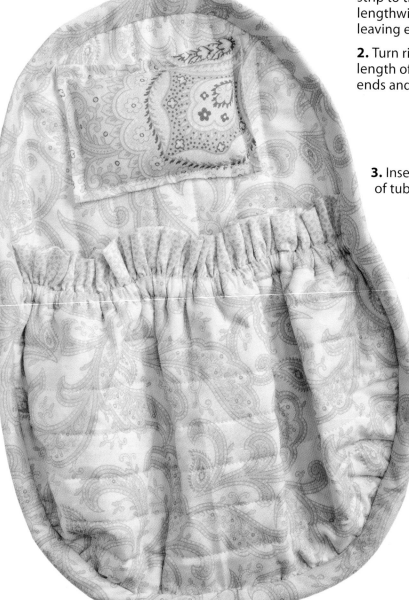

Pretty in Pink

Materials
- 2 coordinating fat quarters (A, B)
- 12 inches ¼-inch-wide gingham ribbon
- 10 inches ¼–½-inch-wide lace edging
- 1 package coordinating ¼-inch-wide single-fold bias tape
- ⅜ x 1½-inch piece fusible hook-and-loop tape
- Coordinating all-purpose thread
- Basic sewing supplies and equipment

Cutting
- Use pattern templates NP1–NP3 (page 48). Fold fat quarters in half, right sides together. Transfer all pattern markings to fabric.

From fabric A:
- Cut one Nightgown Front (NP1) on fold.
- Cut two Nightgown Backs (NP1).

From fabric B:
- Cut one Nightgown Top Yoke Front (NP2) on fold.
- Cut two Nightgown Top Yoke Backs (NP3).

Assembly
Stitch right sides together using a ¼-inch seam allowance unless otherwise specified. Refer to General Instructions (page 2) for finishing all raw edges and for the following construction techniques: Double-Turned ¼-Inch Hem, Gathering, Bias-Tape Bound Edges and Fastener Application.

Nightgown
1. Stitch front yoke (NP3) and back yokes (NP2) together at shoulder seams; press seams open.

2. Stitch ¼ inch from neckline edge. Position lace edging on stitching and pin (Figure 1).

Figure 1

3. Bind the neckline using bias tape, catching the lace in the stitching.

4. Gather top edges of Nightgown Front and Back pieces.

5. Stitch Nightgown Front and Backs to yokes, matching center fronts and backs. Press seams toward yokes.

6. Bind the armhole edges using bias tape.

7. Stitch the side seams.

8. Bind the hemline edge using bias tape.

9. Stitch a Double-Turned ¼-Inch Hem along the center back edges of the Nightgown.

10. Apply fusible hook-and-loop tape fastener to the center back edges of the nightgown.

11. Tie a bow with the gingham ribbon and hand-stitch to the center front of the nightgown just below the bias binding (Figure 2).

Figure 2

Cozy Pajamas

Materials
- 2 coordinating fat quarters (A, B)
- 1 package coordinating ¼-inch-wide single-fold bias tape
- 8 inches ¼-inch-wide elastic
- ⅜ x 1½-inch piece fusible hook-and-loop tape
- Coordinating all-purpose thread
- Basic sewing supplies and equipment

Cutting
- Use pattern templates NP1–NP3 and SP1 (pages 42 and 48). Fold fat quarters in half, right sides together. Transfer all pattern markings to fabric.

From fabric A:
- Cut one Pajama Top Yoke Front (NP2) on fold.
- Cut two Pajama Top Yoke Backs (NP3).
- Cut two Pajama Bottoms (SP1) on fold.

From fabric B:
- Cut one Pajama Top Front (NP1) on fold.
- Cut two Pajama Top Backs (NP1).

Assembly
Stitch right sides together using a ¼-inch seam allowance unless otherwise specified. Refer to General Instructions (page 2) for finishing all raw edges and for the following construction techniques: Bias-Tape Bound Edges, Gathering, Double-Turned ¼-Inch Hem, Elastic Waistline Casing, Bias-Tape Hem and Fastener Application.

Pajama Top:
1. Stitch Pajama Top Yoke Front (NP2) and Back (NP3) together at shoulder seams; press seams open.

2. Gather top edges of Pajama Top Front and Back pieces.

3. Stitch front and backs to yokes, matching center fronts and backs. Press seams toward yokes.

4. Bind neckline and armholes using bias tape.

5. Stitch side seams; press seams toward backs.

6. Bind Pajama Top hemline using bias tape.

7. Stitch a Double-Turned ¼-Inch Hem along back edges of Pajama Top.

8. Apply fusible hook-and-loop tape fastener to Pajama Top Back openings.

Pajama Bottoms

1. Stitch Bias-Tape Hem in Pajama Bottom legs.

2. Stitch center front seam of Pajama Bottoms.

3. Make an Elastic Waistline Casing and thread elastic through the casing, pinning ends of elastic even with the fabric edges.

4. Stitch center back seam.

5. Stitch inner leg seam. ∎

Patterns

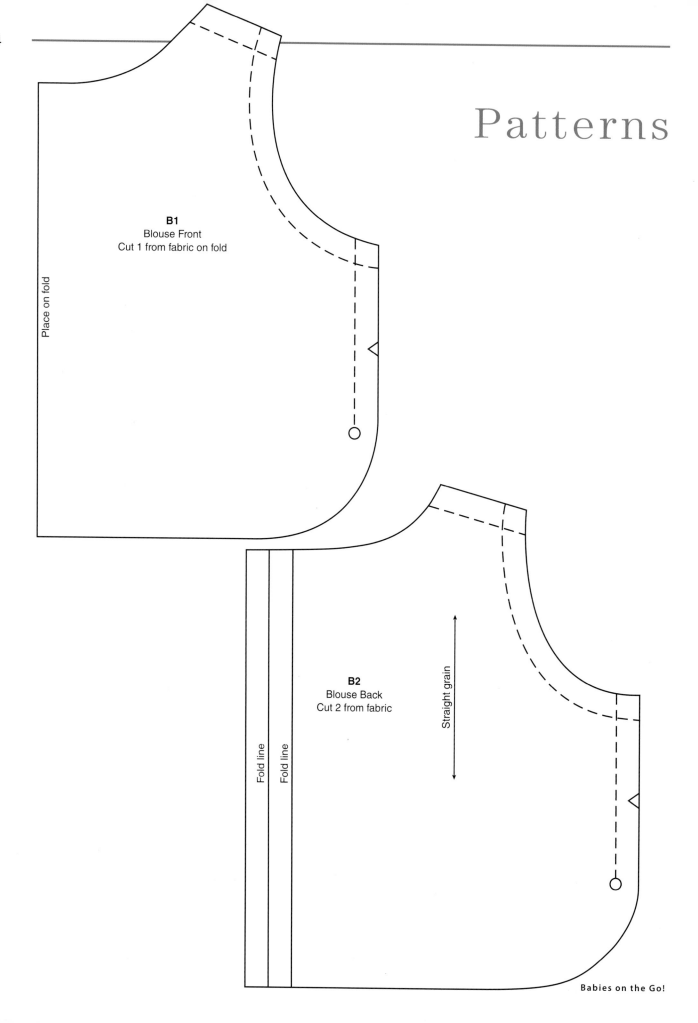

B1
Blouse Front
Cut 1 from fabric on fold

Place on fold

B2
Blouse Back
Cut 2 from fabric

Straight grain

Fold line

Fold line

Babies on the Go!

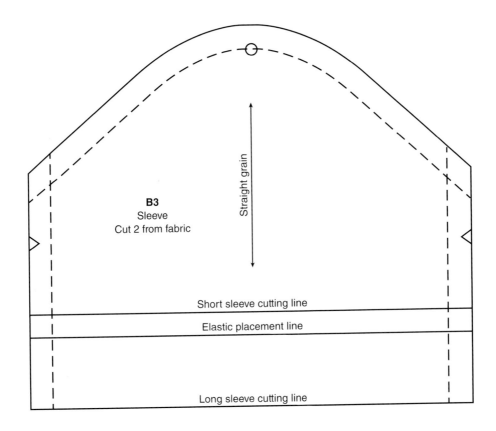

B3
Sleeve
Cut 2 from fabric

Straight grain

Short sleeve cutting line

Elastic placement line

Long sleeve cutting line

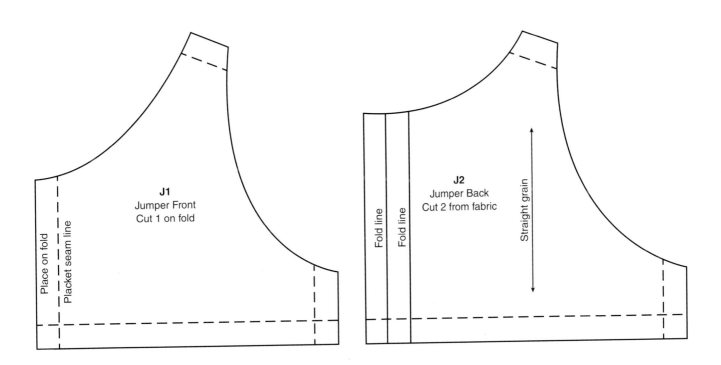

J1
Jumper Front
Cut 1 on fold

Place on fold

Placket seam line

J2
Jumper Back
Cut 2 from fabric

Fold line

Fold line

Straight grain

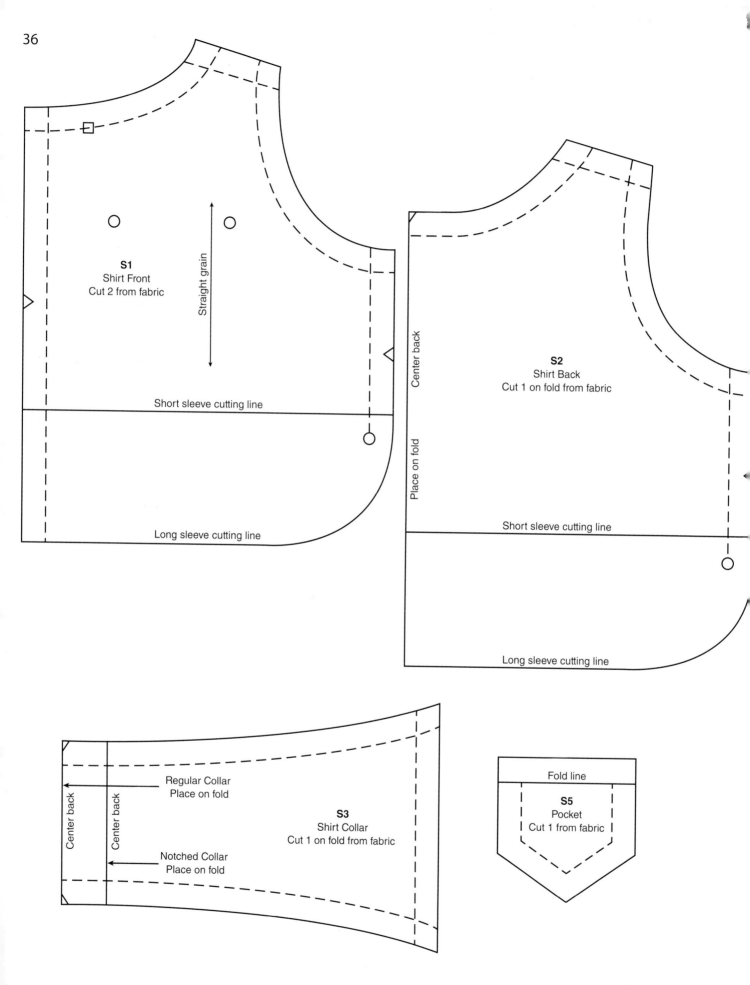

S1
Shirt Front
Cut 2 from fabric

Straight grain

Short sleeve cutting line

Long sleeve cutting line

Center back

Place on fold

S2
Shirt Back
Cut 1 on fold from fabric

Short sleeve cutting line

Long sleeve cutting line

Center back

Center back

Regular Collar
Place on fold

Notched Collar
Place on fold

S3
Shirt Collar
Cut 1 on fold from fabric

Fold line

S5
Pocket
Cut 1 from fabric

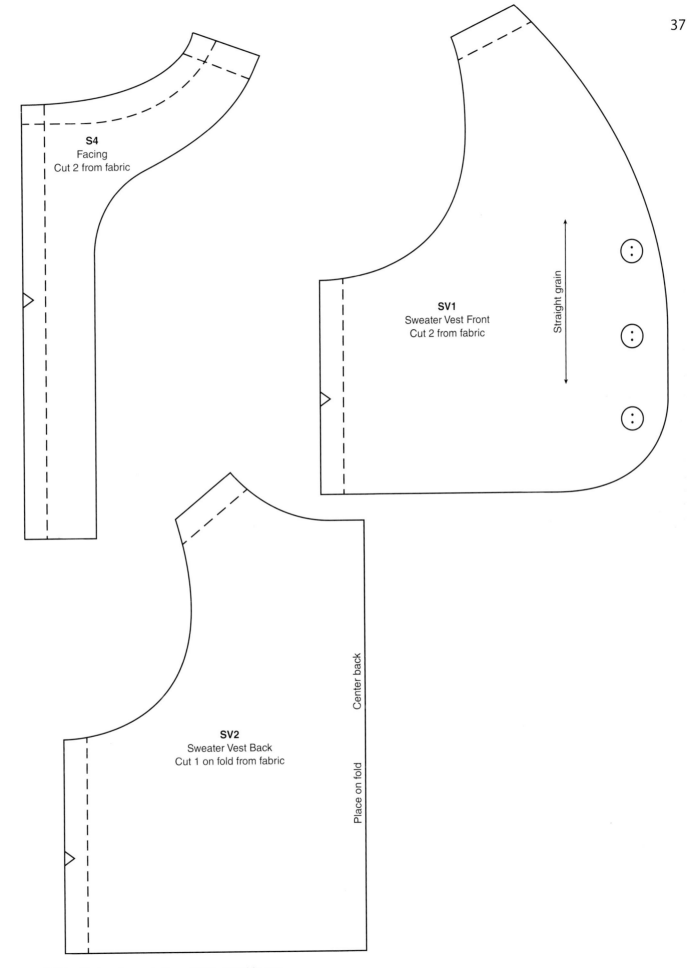

S4
Facing
Cut 2 from fabric

SV1
Sweater Vest Front
Cut 2 from fabric

Straight grain

SV2
Sweater Vest Back
Cut 1 on fold from fabric

Center back

Place on fold

House of White Birches, Berne, Indiana 46711 Clotilde.com

38

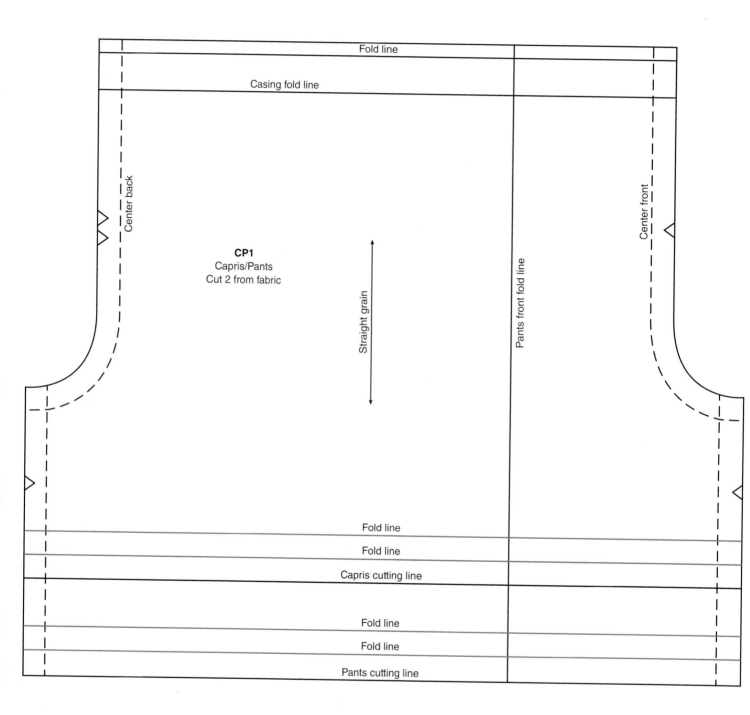

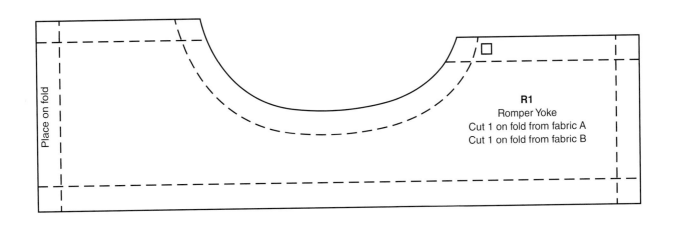

Place on fold

R1
Romper Yoke
Cut 1 on fold from fabric A
Cut 1 on fold from fabric B

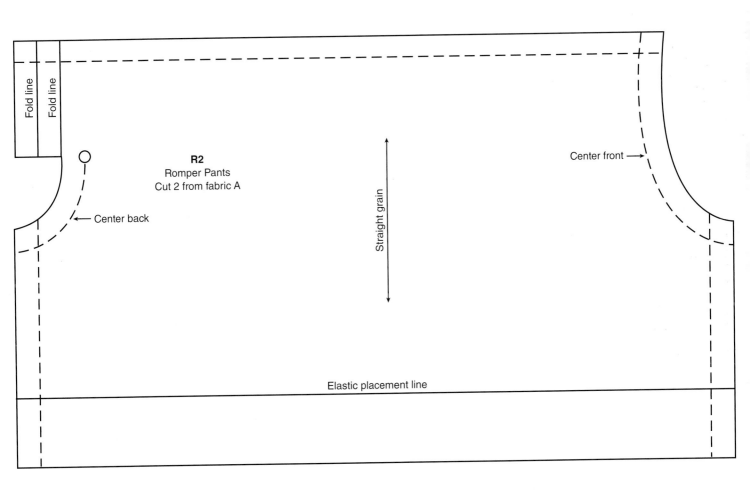

Fold line

Fold line

R2
Romper Pants
Cut 2 from fabric A

Center back

Straight grain

Center front

Elastic placement line

40

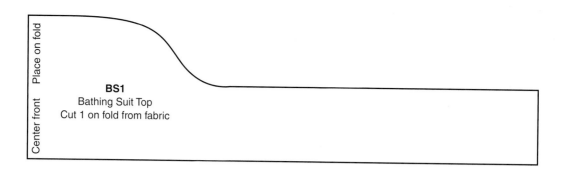

BS1
Bathing Suit Top
Cut 1 on fold from fabric

Center front   Place on fold

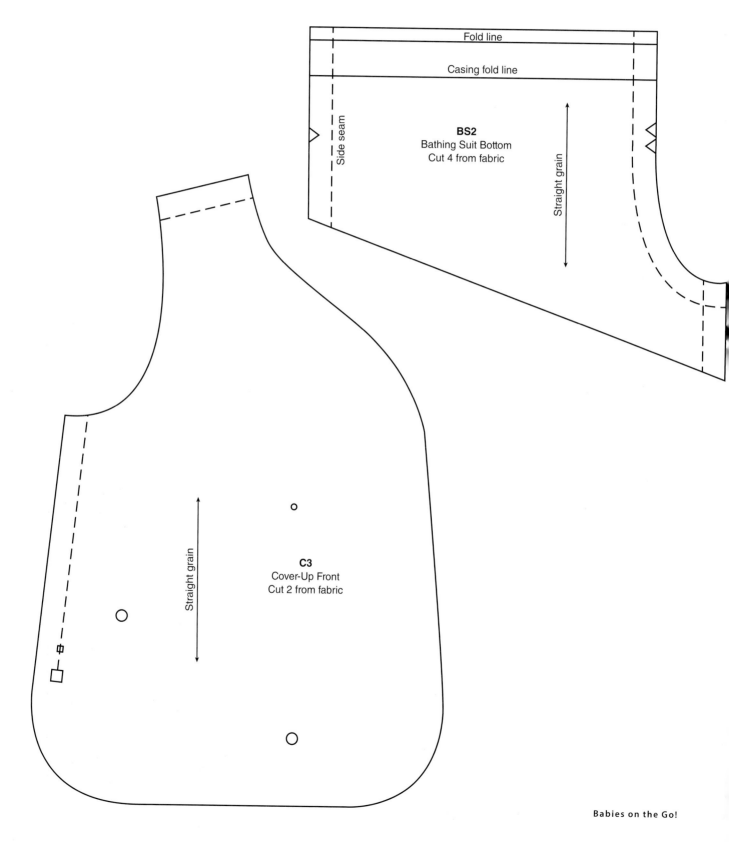

Fold line

Casing fold line

Side seam

BS2
Bathing Suit Bottom
Cut 4 from fabric

Straight grain

C3
Cover-Up Front
Cut 2 from fabric

Straight grain

BS1
Bathing Suit Top

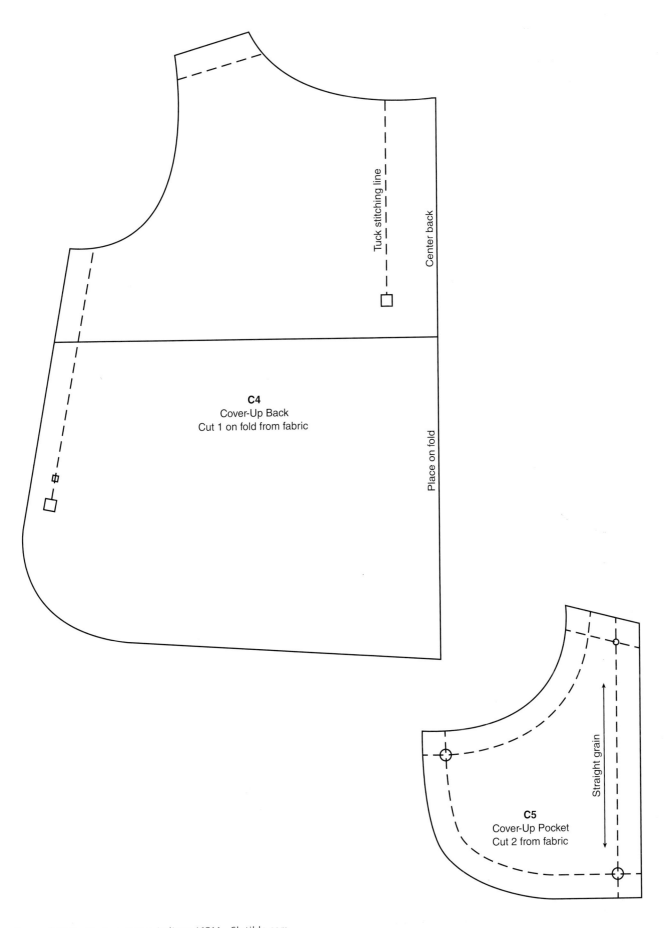

C4
Cover-Up Back
Cut 1 on fold from fabric

Tuck stitching line

Center back

Place on fold

C5
Cover-Up Pocket
Cut 2 from fabric

Straight grain

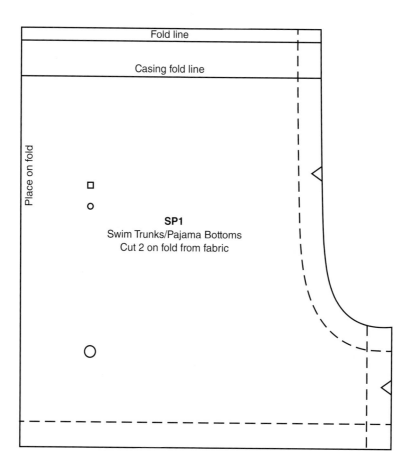

SP1
Swim Trunks/Pajama Bottoms
Cut 2 on fold from fabric

Fold line

Casing fold line

Place on fold

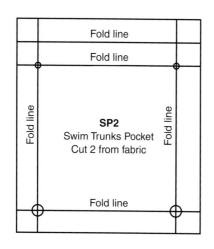

SP2
Swim Trunks Pocket
Cut 2 from fabric

Fold line

Fold line

Fold line

Fold line

Fold line

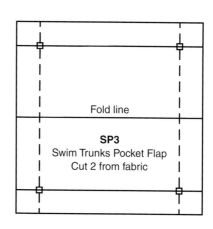

SP3
Swim Trunks Pocket Flap
Cut 2 from fabric

Fold line

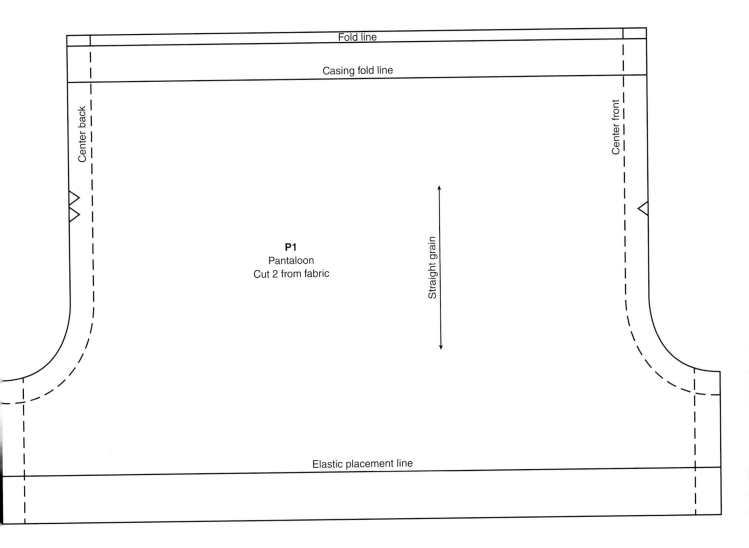

Fold line

Casing fold line

Center back

Center front

P1
Pantaloon
Cut 2 from fabric

Straight grain

Elastic placement line

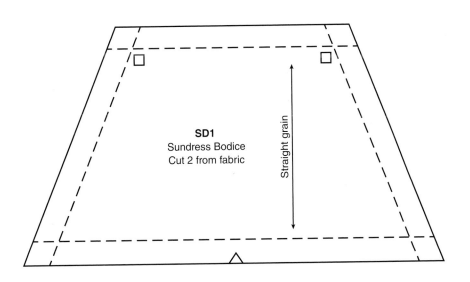

SD1
Sundress Bodice
Cut 2 from fabric

Straight grain

House of White Birches, Berne, Indiana 46711   Clotilde.com

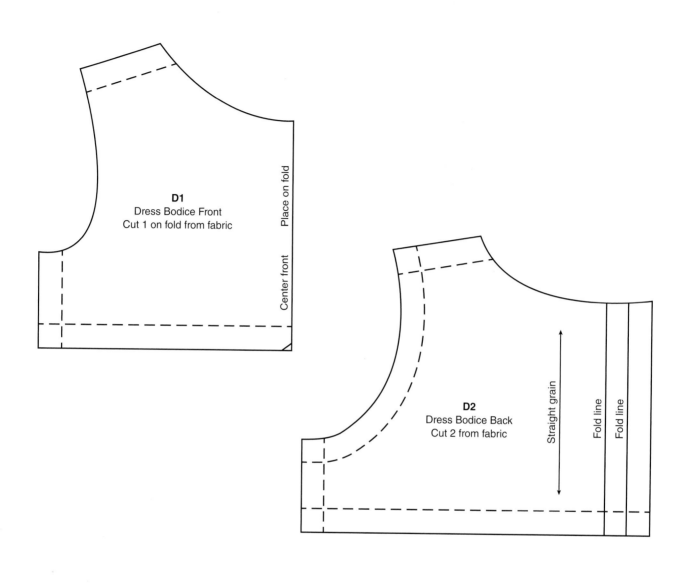

D1
Dress Bodice Front
Cut 1 on fold from fabric

Place on fold

Center front

D2
Dress Bodice Back
Cut 2 from fabric

Straight grain

Fold line

Fold line

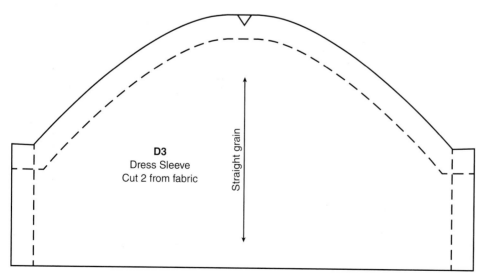

D3
Dress Sleeve
Cut 2 from fabric

Straight grain

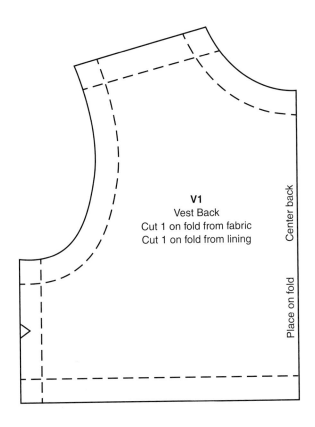

V1
Vest Back
Cut 1 on fold from fabric
Cut 1 on fold from lining

Center back

Place on fold

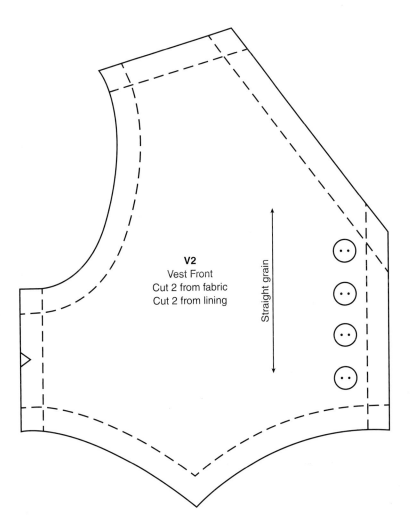

V2
Vest Front
Cut 2 from fabric
Cut 2 from lining

Straight grain

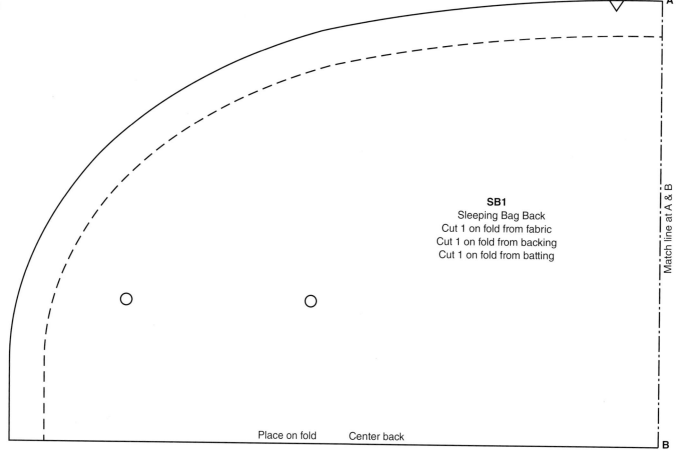

SB1
Sleeping Bag Back
Cut 1 on fold from fabric
Cut 1 on fold from backing
Cut 1 on fold from batting

Match line at A & B

Place on fold   Center back

A

B

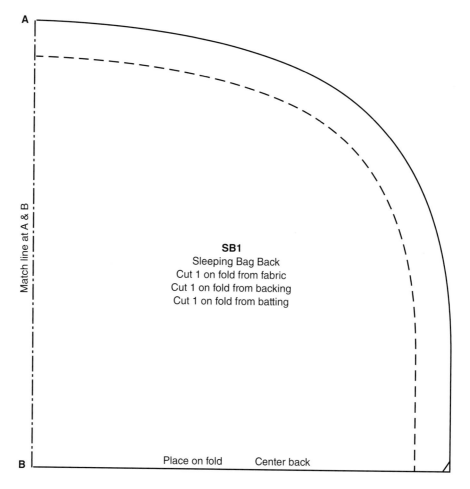

A

Match line at A & B

SB1
Sleeping Bag Back
Cut 1 on fold from fabric
Cut 1 on fold from backing
Cut 1 on fold from batting

B   Place on fold   Center back

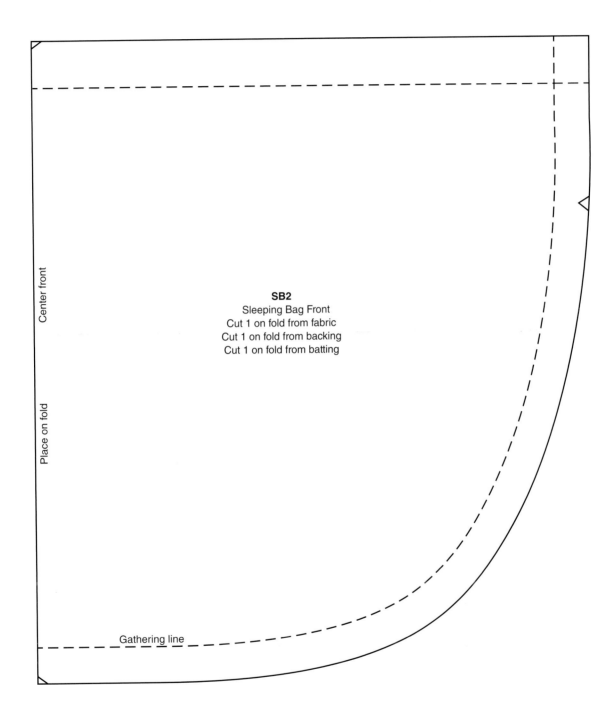

Center front

Place on fold

SB2
Sleeping Bag Front
Cut 1 on fold from fabric
Cut 1 on fold from backing
Cut 1 on fold from batting

Gathering line

House of White Birches, Berne, Indiana 46711   Clotilde.com

48

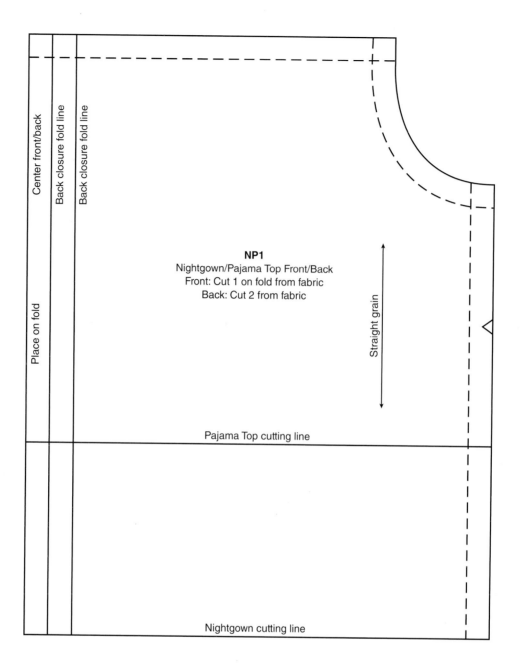

NP1
Nightgown/Pajama Top Front/Back
Front: Cut 1 on fold from fabric
Back: Cut 2 from fabric

Center front/back

Back closure fold line

Back closure fold line

Place on fold

Straight grain

Pajama Top cutting line

Nightgown cutting line

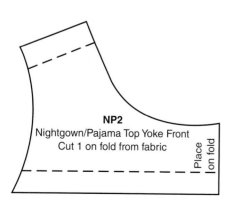

NP2
Nightgown/Pajama Top Yoke Front
Cut 1 on fold from fabric

Place on fold

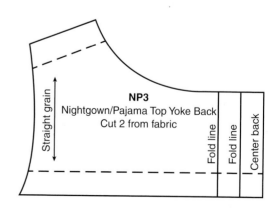

NP3
Nightgown/Pajama Top Yoke Back
Cut 2 from fabric

Straight grain

Fold line

Fold line

Center back